Building a Hacker
Mindset
Cybersecurity Strategies

Table of Contents

Chapter 1. Introduction

In this Special Report titled "Building a Hacker Mindset: Cybersecurity Strategies," we provide digestible yet comprehensive insights into navigating the labyrinth of cyberspace with an invincible armour. Unraveling the intricacies of the digital universe can often feel like deciphering an alien language. But fear not! Our report, masterfully written in jargon-free language, offers a pragmatic look into adopting a hacker's mindset to bolster your cybersecurity. Striking the perfect balance between technical depth and everyday language, this report will guide you step-by-step, enabling you to understand and implement effective cybersecurity strategies. We firmly believe that strong cyber defense is achievable for everyone. Let us inspire you, break down barriers, and illuminate a clearer path in your digital journey. Ready to fortify your online bastions? This report is your secret weapon.

Chapter 2. Understanding the Hacker Mindset

The "hacker mindset" is simply a way of thinking about technology that revolves around innovativeness, curiosity, and persistence. If you strip away the negative connotations usually associated with the term "hacker," you'll find yourself at the essence of what it means: understanding a system—and its weaknesses—better than anyone else.

2.1. Understanding the Basics

To kick start, it's crucial to clarify that not all hackers are malicious. Many hackers seek bugs, holes, and exploits in computer systems out of a sheer passion for understanding and advancing technology. These benevolent hackers are referred to as "white hat" hackers, oftentimes employed to identify vulnerabilities so they can be patched before they're exploited. The darker side of hacking — often referred to as "black hat" hacking — includes individuals or groups who use their skills for harmful or illegal activities.

Understanding the hacker's mindset begins with dispelling preconceived notions about hacking itself. The true essence of hacking focuses on curiosity, a deep desire to understand how things operate, and the creativity to 'think outside the box'. Hacking, in the simplest terms, is the art of exploiting errors or gaps in a system, often disregarded by the average user.

2.2. Mastering Technical Knowledge

A hacker mindset necessitates a strong foundational understanding of the technologies in use. You should be familiar with common operating systems, network structures, and programming languages.

Getting hands-on experience with these systems is essential for comprehending the array of potential attack vectors.

Knowledge doesn't stand still, especially in the digital realm, so continuous learning becomes a part-and-parcel of the hacker mindset. One should embrace changes, updates, and evolution in technologies to stay ahead in this scenario.

Remember to think like a hacker, but act as a protector. Your goal is to identify and remove vulnerabilities before they can be exploited, not to cause harm.

2.3. Developing Cybersecurity Skills

Once you've developed a sound technical foundation, you can start to delve into specific cybersecurity skills. Knowledge of cryptography, a key aspect often used to protect data, is essential. Being aware of various cryptographic algorithms, how they can be cracked and countermeasures for such attacks will lend monumental strength to your cybersecurity arsenal.

Learning about password cracking, phishing, session hijacking, and other common forms of attack helps you anticipate and plan for these attacks. You may also consider learning about more advanced topic areas like Advanced Persistent Threats (APTs), which are typically associated with nation-state actors and involve highly targeted, long-term campaigns against specific organizations.

2.4. Embracing Continuous Learning

Keeping updated on new attack methodologies, latest vulnerability disclosures, and security best practices is an essential component of a hacker's mindset. Subscribe to security newsletters, participate in forums, and don't shy away from enrolling in online courses and webinars. Regularly attending conferences and workshops could also give you a considerable edge.

Engaging with the community also helps you stay connected, providing you with various perspectives and techniques that can improve your approach to securing systems.

2.5. Thinking Creatively To Outsmart Hackers

A fundamental aspect of the hacker's mindset is a relentless curiosity and an innate desire to explore, invent, and uncover new paths. Your knowledge and experience can get you far, but it's your creativity that can help you anticipate the unexpected or seemingly impossible.

Creative thinking is the secret behind many of the greatest hacker discoveries and exploits. It allows you to question the status quo and encourages you to look for vulnerabilities where others might not think to look.

2.6. Developing a Robust Strategy and Ethical Framework

While the hacker mindset is crucial for understanding and identifying vulnerabilities in systems, it's equally important to operate within an ethical framework. Understand existing ethical and legal guidelines surrounding cybersecurity and make sure you're operating within those boundaries.

A robust strategy goes hand in hand with ethical guidelines. Identify critical assets in your system, anticipate potential threats, define what constitutes acceptable risk, and develop a crisis management plan.

Remember, your aim is to strengthen security, not to exploit vulnerabilities for personal gain or to cause harm. Stay ethical, stay curious, and remember that, with a hacker's mindset, you're always learning.

Chapter 3. Cybersecurity Landscape: An Overview

The world of cybersecurity is a dynamic and fast-moving field where threats and defenses continually evolve. It's a digital landscape that can seem overwhelming, but it's vital to understand its broad strokes to draft an effective defense strategy.

3.1. Understanding Cyber Threats

A cyber threat can be understood as the potential for a malicious actor to harm digital systems and data. This might include stealing sensitive information, disrupting digital services, or sabotaging systems and networks. Examples of cyber threats include malware (such as viruses, worms, and ransomware), phishing and spear-phishing attacks, Denial of Service (DoS) attacks, and data breaches.

Threat actors can range from individual criminals to organized criminal groups, state-sponsored attackers, and so-called "hacktivists." Their motivations might be financial gain, military or political advantage, or simply to create chaos.

3.2. Major Cyber Attacks: Illuminating the Threat Landscape

Below are a few noteworthy incidents that serve to highlight the severity and diversity of cyber attacks:

- The WannaCry ransomware attack in May 2017, which affected hundreds of thousands of computers across over 150 countries causing damage estimated in billions of dollars.

- NotPetya malware attack in June 2017, believed to be a state-sponsored attack by Russia against Ukraine, but which also resulted in collateral damage around the world.

- The Yahoo data breaches, discovered in 2016 but dating back to 2013, that exposed personal details of billions of users.

- SolarWinds supply chain attack in 2020 which led to the breach of several US government agencies and large tech companies.

These events serve as a stark reminder of the scale, sophistication, and potential impact of cyber threats.

3.3. Cyber Defense: Meeting Threats Head-on

Cyber defense refers to the measures taken to protect digital assets from threats. This includes the use of technology, processes, and practices designed to protect networks, devices, programs, and data from attack, damage, or unauthorized access. They can relate to elements such as firewalls, vulnerability scanners, intrusion detection systems, etc.

The principle of defense-in-depth suggests deploying multiple layers of security measures to protect the system even if one layer is breached.

3.4. Risk Assessment and Management

Identifying potential threats, vulnerabilities, and impacts is the first step towards effective cyber defense. Once identified, these risks can be managed by implementing controls and measures dictated by the risk or tolerance of the organization to such risks.

3.5. Security Awareness: The Human Factor

People are often the weakest link in security. As such, training and awareness programs are crucial in ensuring that staff members understand the risks and their roles in mitigating them.

3.6. Standards and Regulations

Standards such as the ISO 27000 family and regulations like GDPR for data protection provide guidelines and requirements for organizations to follow to ensure their cybersecurity practices are robust and effective.

3.7. Emerging Trends

With rapid technological advancements, the cybersecurity landscape is constantly changing. AI and machine learning are increasingly used in both cyber attacks and defense. Likewise, as more devices join the IoT network, the surface area for attacks expands.

In conclusion, the cybersecurity landscape is vast, complex, and rapidly changing. Nevertheless, by understanding the types of threats that exist, by implementing sound defenses, assessing and managing risks, increasing security awareness, and adhering to standards and regulations, organizations can significantly bolster their cybersecurity postures. It is vital to stay informed about emerging trends and to be prepared to continually adapt strategies and defenses as the landscape evolves.

Chapter 4. Recognizing Hacker Tactics and Techniques

Understanding the tactics and techniques employed by hackers can greatly improve your skills at identifying and subsequently countering cyber threats. Below is a detailed look into recognized hacker tactics and techniques that commonly pose a significant risk to internet users and systems.

4.1. Social Engineering

Social engineering is one of the most frequently used tactics in a hacker's arsenal. It revolves around manipulating individuals into divulging sensitive information, such as passwords or credit card numbers, or even granting unauthorized access to systems. Hackers often exploit human weaknesses, such as trust and fear, by impersonating trustworthy entities.

Phishing, baiting, and pretexting fall under the umbrella of social engineering:

Phishing involves sending an email that appears to be from a legitimate source (like a bank or a reputable business), directing users to a fake website where they're asked to input sensitive information.

Baiting appeals to a user's curiosity or greed. It could involve leaving a malware-infected USB drive with a label that prompts curiosity in a place where the intended victim is likely to find it.

Pretexting is the act of gathering information through a series of lies. Hackers could create a scenario that coerces the victim into releasing information or performing a particular action that compromises security.

4.2. Password Cracking and Network Intrusion

Password cracking is another hacking method aimed at gaining unauthorized access to systems. Hackers employ various techniques for this:

Brute Force Attacks involve systematically checking all possible passwords until the correct one is found. This method is machine-intensive and can take significant computational power and time.

Dictionary Attacks involve systematically inputting possible passwords drawn from a list of words often used as passwords.

Keylogging involves using a malicious program to record every keystroke made on the victim's keyboard, including passwords.

Rainbow Table Attacks use a precomputed table for reversing cryptographic hash functions to find password hashes and unveil the original passwords.

Once into a system, hackers might employ techniques like **buffer overflow**, which manipulates an application's data handling systems to execute arbitrary code, or use **Rootkit**, a set of software tools that allows unauthorized access to a computer.

4.3. Malware, Viruses, and Trojans

Malware is software designed to infiltrate or harm a computer system without the owner's consent. It includes viruses, worms, Trojan horses, ransomware, spyware, adware, and other malicious programs.

Viruses must be executed to do their damage: they attach themselves to clean files and infect other clean files.

Worms infect networks by exploiting vulnerabilities, often requiring no human intervention to spread.

Trojans appear to be benign programs, but after launching, they execute hidden malicious functions.

Ransomware denies access to a system or data until a ransom is paid. One prevalent ransomware type is 'Cryptolocker,' encrypting victims' files and demanding a digital currency payment to decrypt them.

4.4. Wireless Network Hacking

Wireless Network Hacking involves compromising the security of wireless networks. It includes techniques such as:

Wardriving, which involves driving around and mapping the location of wireless networks.

Evil Twin Attacks, which involve creating a fake wireless network that looks almost identical to a legitimate one to trick users into connecting and revealing sensitive data.

Packet Sniffers capture data passing over the network, which may include sensitive information like passwords and credit card numbers.

Key Cracking involves attackers trying to crack the wireless network's encryption key to gain access to the network.

4.5. Denial of Service (DoS) Attacks

DoS attacks overload system resources, making it inaccessible to the intended users. They often involve bombarding the victim's network with traffic, often from a botnet, which is a group of compromised computers controlled by the hacker.

Distributed Denial-of-Service (DDoS)

In DDoS attacks, the attacker uses multiple computers (usually part of a botnet) to flood the victim's network or website with traffic, taking it offline or slowing it significantly.

4.6. Conclusion

Learning to recognize hacker techniques and tactics is one step toward a stronger cybersecurity posture. By understanding the threats, you can take steps to protect against them, significantly reducing risk. Stay proactive, be informed, and remember that cybersecurity is a continuous journey, not a one-time effort.

Chapter 5. Building Robust Cybersecurity Foundations

Understanding the intricacies of cybersecurity and the importance of creating a robust foundation are paramount to navigating the perilous waters of the digital universe. It all starts with becoming aware of the potential vulnerabilities and learning the measures to safeguard yourself.

=== Understanding the Threat Landscape

Our first step towards a robust cybersecurity foundation is gaining a holistic understanding of the threat landscape. In essence, this refers to the various potential threats found in a digital environment. Undeniably, the sophistication and unpredictability of cyber threats have escalated over the past decade – this includes viruses, worms, ransomware, phishing attacks, Trojans, and more.

A crucial aspect to appreciate is that no entity in the digital realm is immune. Irrespective of the size or sector, every organization or individual is a potential target. The impacts can be vastly different - from the loss of personal data, financial damage, to debilitating reputational harm.

Remember, awareness is not merely about fear – it's about preparedness. By exploring various types of cyber threats, we can anticipate them and shape our defense strategies accordingly.

=== Building Security Consciousness

Developing a security-conscious approach is a key factor in cybersecurity. It pertains to developing habits and practices that prioritize security. This mindset should ideally be promoted at every level, from c-suite executives to interns.

Encouraging cybersecurity education, incorporating best practices such as developing strong passwords, regular system updates, backing up data, and avoiding suspicious links, can enormously contribute to an entity's cyber resilience.

In the end, a robust cybersecurity foundation isn't exclusively about technology; it's as much about people and behavioral change.

Making Use of Reliable Security Frameworks

Cybersecurity frameworks provide an outline of best practices that an organization or an individual can use to manage their cyber risks. These are typically designed by renowned cybersecurity authorities and offer a step-by-step guide to building a secure infrastructure.

Adopting the right framework for your specific needs can lead to improved security. Examples include NIST (National Institute of Standards & Technology) Cybersecurity Framework, ISO 27001/27002 Security Framework, and CIS (Center for Internet Security) Controls.

Each of these frameworks is catered to a different purpose, thus, understanding your specific requirements will guide you in selecting the appropriate framework.

The Importance of Regular Auditing and Risk Assessment

Regular auditing and risk assessment are vital in maintaining a dynamic cybersecurity posture. This refers to the periodic scrutiny of systems, practices, and procedures.

Risk assessment helps identify potential vulnerabilities and measure their potential impacts. This evaluation allows the creation of prioritized action plans, providing clear visibility into where resources are needed most.

Audits, on the other hand, offer a comprehensive view of the end-to-end state of security. They check the adherence to various policies and standards, ensuring that the safeguards are operating as expected.

Reaction: Incident Response and Recovery

Any cybersecurity strategy is incomplete without an incident response and recovery plan. It outlines the procedures to follow in the aftermath of a cyber attack, reducing the extent of damage and quickening recovery.

This plan should involve the identification of compromised areas, containment of breach, eradication of the threat, recovery measures, and finally, lessons learned from the incident. Remember, the speed and accuracy of the response can significantly determine the impact of a cybersecurity event.

Continuous Learning and Adaptation

Cybersecurity is a dynamic field, continually evolving with the threat landscape. Hence, a staunch commitment to continual learning and adaptation is essential.

Organizational resilience in cybersecurity relies not only on established defenses but also its ability to respond to and evolve with the changing tactics of cybercriminals.

To conclude, building a robust cybersecurity foundation is a holistic proposition encompassing awareness, security consciousness, usage of established frameworks, regular audits and risk assessment, a solid incident response plan, and a commitment to continual learning.

Remember, it doesn't always have to be a battle; consider it as a dance with the adversaries. Maneuver the digital space with grace and enjoy the dance while the fort holds strong.

Chapter 6. Risk Assessment: Identifying Your Vulnerabilities

In this unpredictable cyberspace where threats continue to evolve with daunting speed, the paramount importance of risk assessment cannot be overemphasized. Risk assessment is the process of identifying and analysing potential issues that could negatively impact key business initiatives or critical projects in order to fashion out effective and efficient strategies to prevent them.

6.1. Understanding Risk Assessment

Risk assessment is predicated on a simple understanding - you cannot protect everything equally. In this vein, understanding which assets are truly critical to your organization is the first step in building a realistic and cost-effective defense strategy. An effective risk assessment process should identify, prioritize, and estimate the risks to which your business is most susceptible.

Establishing a well-structured risk assessment process within your organization involves identification of hazards, analysis to understand the potential risks associated to these hazards, and evaluation on whether existing control measures are sufficient or if more should be done to mitigate them. It's a cyclic process, involving regular checks, with adjustments made as necessary to accommodate changes in circumstances.

6.2. Key Elements of Risk Assessment

Risk assessments break down into four key areas:

1. Threat Assessment: Recognizing and documenting potential threats.

2. Vulnerability Assessment: Evaluating your assets for any weaknesses that could be exploited.

3. Impact Assessment: Determining possible consequences should a threat capitalize on a vulnerability.

4. Risk Analysis: Weighing the potential costs, in terms of tangibles like money and intangibles like reputation or trust, against the potential benefits of allowing certain risks.

6.3. The Process of Risk Assessment

Risk assessment constitutes three key steps: identification, estimation, and prioritization of potential risks. Here's how you can go about each:

1. Identification: This involves pinpointing what threats could affect your organization's assets. These might be software vulnerabilities, data theft, or employee errors, among others.

2. Estimation: Once threats have been identified, estimating their likelihood helps determine how much to invest in preventing them. Metrics used for this estimation could include historical data, industry patterns, and expert opinions.

3. Prioritization: Finally, risks should be prioritized based on their estimated impact and likelihood. This ranking allows organizations to focus their mitigation efforts on the highest-ranked risks.

6.4. Conducting a Risk Assessment

Having understood the importance and basic framework of risk assessments, it's now time to take a look at how these assessments can be effectively conducted.

1. Assemblage of an Expert Team: The first step in conducting a risk assessment is to assemble a team of individuals who have a deep understanding of the company and its workings. This team should have representatives from various departments.

2. Listing and Analysing Assets: The team's first task will be to identify all assets that need protecting. This includes everything from tangible assets like hardware and physical infrastructure, to intangible assets like data and brand reputation.

3. Identifying Threats: From this understanding, the team must identify potential threats to these assets. Threats can be internal (like employee errors or insubordination) or external (like cybercriminals or natural disasters).

4. Documenting Vulnerabilities: After identifying threats, the team must identify vulnerability points within the system that these threats could exploit. Assessment tools exist to aid in this process of vulnerability identification.

5. Determining the Potential Impact: Each threat-vulnerability pair should be evaluated for its potential impact on the organization. The team must think critically about possible consequences and the potential cost of those outcomes.

6. Mitigation Strategies: Based on the findings, the team needs to design mitigation strategies. Strategies must be chosen according to their potential effectiveness, cost, and the organization's specific priorities and values.

7. Regular Review: As the digital landscape evolves, so do its dangers. It is therefore critical to regularly review and update risk assessments.

6.5. The Power of Tools and Frameworks

Organizations have an arsenal of tools and frameworks at their disposal to conduct efficient risk assessments. Some of the most popular ones include:

1. OCTAVE: A framework created by CERT/CC, OCTAVE (Operationally Critical Threat, Asset, and Vulnerability Evaluation) looks at organizational and technological aspects of risk.

2. FAIR: The Factor Analysis of Information Risk (FAIR) is a quantitative model that uses loss event frequency and magnitude as its cornerstone for evaluating risk.

3. Risk Matrix: This is a tool used for risk assessment that visually represents risks in terms of their likelihood and impact.

Using these tools can simplify the risk assessment process and make it more structured and repeatable. It's important to choose tools and frameworks that best align with your organization's needs and capabilities.

6.6. Conclusion

In conclusion, risk assessment may appear a daunting process, especially given the breadth and constant evolution of the digital universe. But remember, the main goal is not to eliminate every conceivable risk – an impossible task – but rather to understand the organization's risk landscape in such detail as to make informed strategic decisions. Risk is intrinsic to growth and innovation, and understanding it is the first step in controlling it. Remember, in cybersecurity strategy, knowledge is the best defence.

Remember to stay abreast of new developments in cybersecurity, continue assessing and reassessing your threats, and most importantly, keep fostering a culture of security awareness in your team. Your human assets, when empowered with the right knowledge, are the greatest weapon in your arsenal against cyber threats.

Chapter 7. Developing Effective Cybersecurity Strategies

Having a strong cybersecurity strategy goes beyond installing the most expensive firewall or antivirus software. It implicates understanding cyber threats, creating policies to address these threats, and ensuring organizational readiness against potential cyber-attacks. Let's embark on a journey to develop effective cybersecurity strategies.

7.1. Understanding the Threat Landscape

Cyber threats evolve at an alarming rate, escalating the importance of understanding the threat landscape. This is your first step towards developing an effective cybersecurity strategy.

Identifying threats requires a consistent review of global trends and frequent security assessments of your system. Various online security resources, such as cybersecurity blogs, forums, professional networks, and official announcements by government security agencies, can provide the necessary information.

Begin by closely monitoring specific threats relevant to your organization. What are the most common types of attacks seen in your industry? From phishing attacks to ransomware, it's crucial to know what you're up against.

Remember, knowledge is power. The more you learn about these threats, the easier it becomes to craft defenses.

7.2. Creating a Risk Assessment Framework

A risk assessment framework allows you to identify the most vulnerable aspects of your digital infrastructure. It's a personalized, sophisticated tool that considers various factors such as your company's operational model, geographic location, stakeholder interactions, nature of stored data, and industry-specific threats.

The risk assessment framework should be clear, usable, and thorough. Make sure to involve all relevant stakeholders when creating it as this will improve its effectiveness.

7.3. Establishing Cybersecurity Policies and Procedures

Once you comprehend your threat landscape and have assessed the potential risks, the next step is establishing cybersecurity policies and procedures.

These should be in a document that is easily accessible to all employees and includes an acceptable use policy, a password policy, an incident response policy, and a disaster recovery plan.

An acceptable use policy clarifies which behaviours are considered acceptable and unacceptable when using company devices or networks. From proper email usage to appropriate web browsing, it helps maintain a baseline for appropriate actions.

The password policy should detail password complexity requirements, change periodicity, and other practices. If you opt for multi-factor authentication, make sure to include it.

A detailed incident response plan is essential to outline the necessary steps following a security incident, helping to minimize damage and downtime. An exhaustive disaster recovery plan should be in place for worst-case scenarios, ensuring your operations can continue while minimizing any potential data loss.

7.4. Cybersecurity Education and Awareness

Training employees to recognise potential threats and respond accordingly is an integral part of any cybersecurity strategy. From simple phishing emails to sophisticated social engineering attacks, the human element can often be the weakest link in your cybersecurity.

Launching regular security awareness programs and conducting employee training sessions can significantly mitigate risks. Topics should range from how to spot suspicious emails to the appropriate handling of sensitive data.

7.5. Choosing the Right Cybersecurity Tools

Choosing tools for your cybersecurity stack is a vital part of your strategy. Strike a balance between cost and effectiveness while selecting tools.

Firewalls, antivirus software, intrusion detection/prevention solutions (IDS/IPS), and data leakage prevention (DLP) tools are just a few from a vast pool. Each offers different security features, but it's beneficial to have a mix of tools to have comprehensive coverage.

7.6. Partnering with External Services

Sometimes, the best strategy includes seeking external help. Professional cybersecurity service providers can offer specialized advice, manage cybersecurity on your behalf or provide post-incident investigation.

When selecting a provider, look for services specific to your needs, their experience level, industry knowledge, and cost.

7.7. Continual Monitoring and Review

Lastly, your cybersecurity strategy should include a process for continual monitoring and review. It allows for the speedy detection of breaches and prompt reaction to minimize damage.

Regular audits provide an opportunity to refine your strategy, incorporate new threats, and ensure that your systems and procedures remain effective over time.

Building a hacker mindset isn't about becoming a master at hacking but understanding how such minds operate. By developing an effective cyber-security strategy, you guard against these unseen threats and ensure the safety of your digital universe.

Chapter 8. Phishing, Malware, and Ransom Attacks: A Close Look

Cybersecurity threats come in various types, each functioning with unique strategies, all geared towards undermining your digital safety. In our multi-faceted exploration into these cyber threats, we focus on phishing, malware, and ransom attacks, which continue to plague the digital world.

8.1. Understanding Phishing

Phishing remains one of the most potent cyber threats, cleverly masked behind the facade of legitimacy. The attacker poses as a trusted entity and sends messages or emails, tricking victims into revealing sensitive data. These data, often comprising bank account details, credit card numbers, and passwords, are then used for fraudulent activities.

To recognize phishing attempts, one must note several red flags. Phishing emails often engender a sense of urgency, forcing you to act swiftly. They could contain spelling and grammar mistakes. A careful look at the email address may reveal that it is not from the purported organization. Always be cautious about emails requesting sensitive data, as genuine organizations seldom ask for such information via email.

8.2. Fortifying Defenses Against Phishing

Strong defenses against phishing are a combination of education, technology, and cautious online behavior. Foremost is awareness. Be wary of unsolicited communications and unfamiliar sources. A rule of thumb is, "When in doubt, throw it out!"

On the technological end, install anti-phishing toolbars and regularly update your browsers. These toolbars compare websites you visit against known phishing sites and alert you. In addition, ensure that your systems and software are always up-to-date, fortifying your system against known vulnerabilities.

Also, try to avoid clicking on links in emails. Instead, go directly to the source's website by typing their real URL into the browser.

8.3. Unveiling Malware Threats

Next, we embark on an exploration of malware, an all-encompassing term used to define malicious software designed to infiltrate, damage, or disable computers, computer networks, or gain access to crucial, often sensitive, personal information.

Malware comes in several forms, including viruses, worms, trojans, spyware, adware, and ransomware. Each has a unique way of corrupting your system. Viruses, for example, attach themselves to clean files and infect other clean files. Worms exploit security flaws to spread across networks, while Trojans disguise themselves as legitimate software.

8.4. Tactics to Combat Malware

There are numerous strategies for deflecting malware threats. Firstly, it's vital to install a robust and reliable antivirus program that can detect and quarantine malware before it wreaks havoc. Regularly update your antivirus software for it to recognize new malware.

More critically, observe safe internet use habits. Don't install software from untrusted sources, and stay aware of what you click. If a deal looks too good to be true, it might be a trap laid by cybercriminals.

Always back up your files since malware can wipe your data. Regular backups mean that even if your system is compromised, you can quickly restore your information.

8.5. Dismantling Ransomware

Lastly, we will delve into ransomware, a particularly malignant form of malware. Ransomware encrypts victim's files, with the attacker demanding a ransom in exchange for the decryption key.

Ransomware can infiltrate your systems via malicious email attachments, infected software applications, and external storage devices. Some types exploit security holes without the victim having to do anything.

8.6. Defending Against Ransomware

Fighting ransomware is a matter of preventive and responsive measures. Using reliable security software and keeping it up-to-date can prevent many ransomware attempts. Implement email filters to catch and quarantine suspicious emails, and disable macros to prevent automatic execution of malicious codes.

Regular data backups are crucial. If you are targeted by a ransomware attack, a backup will allow the restoration of your files without paying a ransom.

However, prevention isn't always foolproof. If struck by ransomware, isolate the infected machine from the network to prevent the spread. Report the incident to your local authorities and engage professional help. Lastly, remember that paying the ransom is not recommended. There's no guarantee that you'll receive the decryption key, and it lures cybercriminals into continuing their illicit activities.

With the ever-evolving nature of cyber threats, maintaining a robust defense mechanism will require consistent learning, vigilance, and proactive measures. While adopting this 'hacker mindset,' you'll be able to navigate the often tumultuous cyberspace while ensuring safety and integrity.

Chapter 9. Incident Response: Dealing with a Breach

Many people liken getting hacked to contracting a disease. It's altering, invasive, and throws things into disarray. But it's not all gloom and doom. Having a robust incident response plan in place can greatly mitigate the adverse effects of a breach and ensure an efficient recovery.

9.1. Understanding Incident Response

Incident response is a structured methodology for handling security incidents, breaches, and cyber threats. A well-defined incident response plan allows you to effectively identify, minimize the damage, and reduce the cost of a cyber attack, while finding and fixing the issue that caused the breach.

1. Preparation: This is your first line of defense. Establish policies, procedures, and collaborate with stakeholders to determine an effective approach to cyber threats. Regular training and threat simulations can prepare your team for potential incidents.

2. Identification: Here, it's about early detection. Efficient and proactive monitoring systems can prompt warnings when discrepancies are detected.

3. Containment: Once a breach has been identified, the priority is containment to prevent further compromise. This could involve isolating affected systems or temporarily shutting down services.

4. Eradication: The eradication phase involves removing the threat from the compromised systems, which may involve patches, software updates, or changing compromised user credentials.

5. Recovery: This phase ensures systems are restored to their regular functions and readied for business as usual. It may require extensive tests and monitoring to ensure a secure environment.

6. Lessons Learnt: Post-incident analysis is vital. It identifies the root cause, fixes vulnerabilities, and aids in refining your incident response strategy.

9.2. Creating a Cybersecurity Incident Response Team

The lifeline of an incident response process is a dedicated Cybersecurity Incident Response Team (CIRT). These professionals identify the incidents, respond to them, and ensure they do not recur.

- Team leader: Oversees the response process, assigns tasks, and acts as the point of contact.

- Incident responders: Deep-dive into the technical aspects, decipher the threat, and strategize responses.

- IT professionals: Fix the infrastructure issues, patch the vulnerabilities, and restore systems.

- Communications team: Handles internal and external communications, providing relevant and timely updates on the situation.

9.3. Incident Detection and Analysis

Identifying a breach can be like looking for a needle in a haystack. The key is recognizing what constitutes an incident. Suspicious activity patterns, unusual data transfers, or sudden system failures could indicate a potential breach.

Security Information and Event Management (SIEM) systems can provide useful insights into security logs and offer a comprehensive view of your network's security events. Regular audits and network traffic analysis can help detect any anomalies prompting a threat.

9.4. Containment and Neutralization

Once a breach is identified, swift containment actions are required. Isolating affected devices from the network can prevent propagation. Remember, a quick response can significantly limit the damage.

Neutralization involves removing malware, blocking compromised user accounts, and patching vulnerabilities. Given the complexity and persistence of modern cyber threats, multiple iterations may be needed to fully eliminate some threats.

9.5. Post-Breach Recovery and Learning from Incidents

After containment and eradication, recovery measures are initiated. This involves restoring and validating services systematically to ensure no backdoors are left open, and normal operations can resume safely.

An incident should always be a learning opportunity. Post-incident review identifies potential weaknesses in your system and policies. It's also a time to reflect on the efficacy of your response, polish your strategy, and adjust the protocol accordingly.

9.6. Incident Response Tools

Having a suitable suite of tools can greatly enhance your incident response efficiency.

- Forensic tools: Identify and analyze the nature of the attack. This could include antivirus programs and specialized forensics software.

- Ticketing tools: Facilitate communication and coordinate response activities.

- Incident management platforms: Provide an overview of response activities and track key performance indicators.

Strengthening your cybersecurity is a never-ending process. It's a complex task that requires widespread awareness, regular reviews, and constant upgrades to stay ahead of evolving threats. But with a solid incident response strategy, a well-equipped team, and an informed organization, you can face future cyber threats head-on, reducing both their likelihood and potential damage.

Chapter 10. Maintaining and Updating Your Cybersecurity Strategy

As with any strategy, your approach to cybersecurity involves continuous review and recalibration as your business and technologies evolve, and as new threats emerge. This process isn't static, it is a constant ebb and flow requiring vigilance, proactivity, and a keen understanding of cyber trends.

10.1. Understanding the Hacker Mindset

To fortify your system, it helps to think like a potential intruder. Placing yourself in an attacker's mindset will help you identify vulnerabilities in your system that you may not have noticed from a defensive standpoint. This approach helps in identifying potential security breaches and ensures you stay one step ahead, making it harder for attacks to penetrate your digital defense.

In the realm of cybersecurity, it's crucial to remember that hackers often exploit human elements, not just system vulnerabilities. Employees are targeted via various methods such as phishing, social engineering, and even through physical access control systems. So make sure to educate your employees about potential threats and how to counteract them.

10.2. Updating Your Cybersecurity Strategy

Ensuring your cybersecurity strategy remains effective in the long run involves regular audits and updates. This necessitates a close look at your current security measures, understanding their strengths, and identifying areas for improvement. Also, take into account the most recent threats and the direction in which digital security is heading.

The speed at which cybersecurity technology evolves outpaces standard update cycles. To keep up, security systems should be updated regularly and in line with the release of new patches and software. If your business uses custom software or systems that require manual updates, be sure to establish a routine or protocol for this. Failure to update can leave your systems vulnerable to attacks that could have otherwise been avoided.

10.3. Embracing Emerging Technologies

Technologies such as AI (Artificial Intelligence), ML (Machine Learning), and Blockchain have exhibited immense potential in the realm of cybersecurity. AI and ML can help detect and deter cyber-attacks in their infancy, while blockchain technology can help ensure the integrity and security of data.

Leveraging these technologies in your cybersecurity strategy can offer a robust, more resilient defense line. However, incorporating such innovations in your strategy involves a careful understanding of how they work and what value they bring to your business. Investing in the necessary training and consultation can ensure they are implemented effectively.

10.4. Achieving Regulatory Compliance

A substantial part of maintaining and updating your cybersecurity strategy involves staying compliant with relevant regulations and industry standards. Whether it's GDPR (General Data Protection Regulation) for businesses handling European data, or HIPAA (Health Insurance Portability and Accountability Act) for healthcare industries, these guidelines provide a standard to follow for enhancing security and protecting customers' data.

Changes to these regulations necessitate modifications to your cybersecurity strategy, so it's essential to keep abreast of these updates. Failing to meet these standards not only exposes your systems to vulnerabilities but may also result in penalties, adding a financial cost to the already damaging effects of a potential breach.

10.5. Training and Education

User error contributes significantly to successful cyber-attacks. A well-trained staff can serve as the first line of defense against various types of cyber security threats. Conduct regular training sessions, and ensure that all employees can recognize and respond to threats such as phishing emails, scams, and other types of social engineering.

Also, training should be provided for the proper use of technologies, especially as they evolve or change. Even your most advanced systems will be rendered useless without a workforce that understands how to use them.

10.6. Continual Improvement

Cybersecurity is a journey and not a destination. The landscape evolves constantly, and the threats evolve with it. The key to maintaining a robust cybersecurity strategy lies in the continuous improvement of your defenses in accordance with the emerging trends and threats. Reflect regularly on the efficacy of your strategy and be prepared to adjust as needed.

In conclusion, updating and maintaining your cybersecurity strategy is a vital, ongoing process. By embracing a hacker's mindset, regularly updating your strategy and technology, achieving regulatory compliance, and investing in continual training, your business can stay one step ahead, navigating the dynamic landscape of cyberspace securely and confidently.

Chapter 11. The Future of Cybersecurity: Predictions and Preparations

In the realm of digital technology, where evolution is the only constant, the future of cybersecurity stands on the threshold of exciting and daunting developments. As we chart a path into uncharted territories, keeping eyes peeled towards the horizon will prepare you, the digital voyagers, for the looming Pandora's Box of cyber threats.

11.1. Anticipated Cyber Threats

Going by the current trends, ransomware and phishing will continue wreaking havoc. But the specter of quantum computing looms large, potentially rendering the current cryptographic systems obsolete. AI algorithms entrusted with enormous quantities of sensitive data pose another significant concern.

Ransomware, where attackers encrypt data and demand a ransom for its release, is increasingly targeting larger organizations and critical infrastructure. The cost, both monetary and operational, is staggering, bringing corporations and governments to their knees.

Phishing scams exploiting human gullibility continue to be a favorite among hackers. When emails masquerading as legitimate communication trick you into divulging sensitive data, the consequences can be disastrous.

Quantum computers exploit the peculiarities of quantum physics to perform calculations at speeds unachievable by today's computers. If a hacker masters this technology, the current cryptographic systems will crumble, opening floodgates of sensitive and confidential data.

AI-based systems are growing both in sophistication and prevalence. Yet, misuse of such algorithms could covertly introduce bias into the decision-making process or breach privacy, giving rise to dire implications.

11.2. Cybersecurity Toolbox: Future Edition

A robust defense mechanism for the above threats necessitates revising our cybersecurity toolbox. Machine Learning (ML) and Artificial Intelligence (AI) will enable anomaly detection in network traffic, flagging unusual patterns and trends.

Blockchains, the underlying technology of cryptocurrency, can facilitate secure transactions by decentralizing data and creating unhackable ledgers.

Quantum cryptography and post-quantum cryptography are other avenues explored to counter quantum threats. While the former uses quantum physics for key distribution, the latter focuses on cryptographic algorithms that resist quantum attacks. These two strategies, used together, will be the cornerstone of future cryptographic systems.

Lastly, for human-induced threats like phishing, continuous education and fostering a cyber-secure culture can serve as powerful deterrents.

11.3. The Quantum Conundrum

The race is on to build functional and scalable quantum computers worldwide. As with all powerful tools, the impact will largely depend on who gains access and what their intent is. However, the implications for cybersecurity are twofold.

Despite the threats it poses, quantum computing can also be the very weapon to protect us. Quantum key distribution and quantum entanglement, futuristic pillars of cryptography, promise nearly unhackable communication channels.

11.4. AI's Double-Edged Sword

AI, while making systems smarter and autonomous, can also make them increasingly susceptible to manipulation. Notably, the threat involves 'adversarial attacks', where a malicious actor feeds misleading input to the AI, causing it to make harmful decisions.

Yet, the same AI can build defences never dreamed of before. By sifting through vast network logs, advanced AI models can spot minute anomalies and trends that humans might miss, nipping in the bud potential cyber threats.

11.5. Trust No One: Zero Trust

The concept of 'Zero Trust' will likely gain massive traction, predicated on the principle 'never trust, always verify.' This model advocates a holistic approach where trust is not decided by the network's perimeter. Instead, every entity, be it users, devices or network components, should be verified regardless of their location or network connection.

11.6. Regulations for the Win

New laws and regulatory frameworks must be iterative, grappling in real-time with the rapid technological shifts. Stricter data protection and privacy rules along with harsher penalties for cybercrimes should serve as significant deterrents. Significant efforts should be directed towards promoting global cooperation, which will be paramount in any fight against cyber threats.

A future-ready cybersecurity ethos requires you to stay informed about emerging threats, equip yourself with developing technologies, and embrace updated regulations. Being prepared today for the uncertainties of tomorrow is your best defence. Let us continue to build, block by block, a robust defence wall against the rising tide of cyber threats.

www.ingramcontent.com/pod-product-compliance
Lightning Source LLC
La Vergne TN
LVHW051625050326
832903LV00033B/4673